Fancy Free

Poems selected by Dennis Saunders
Photographs by Terry Williams

Evans Brothers Limited London

Published by Evans Brothers Limited,
Montague House, Russell Square,
London, W.C.1.

First published 1974
Reprinted 1976, 1978

Set in Century by Photoprint Plates Limited, Rayleigh, Essex,
and printed in Great Britain by Sackville Press, Billericay Ltd.,
Billericay.

ISBN 0 237 4408 4   PRA 6125

Contents

Sea and Shore

Index of Authors

Index of first lines

Creatures Small

Hurt no living thing

Hurt no living thing;
Ladybird, nor butterfly,
Nor moth with dusty wing,
Nor cricket chirping cheerily,
Nor grasshopper so light of leap,
Nor dancing gnat, nor beetle fat,
Nor harmless worms that creep.

Christina Rossetti

The cat

Within that porch, across the way,
I see two naked eyes this night;
Two eyes that neither shut nor blink,
Searching my face with a green light.

But cats to me are strange, so strange—
I cannot sleep if one is near;
And though I'm sure I see those eyes,
I'm not so sure a body's there!

W. H. Davies

The prayer of the mouse

I am so little and grey,
dear God,
how can You keep me in mind?
Always spied upon,
always chased.
Nobody ever gives me anything,
and I nibble meagrely at life.
Why do they reproach me with being a mouse?
Who made me but You?
I only ask to stay hidden.
Give me my hunger's pittance
safe from the claws
of that devil with green eyes.

Amen

Carmen Bernos de Gasztold

The bat

By day the bat is cousin to the mouse.
He likes the attic of an aging house.

His fingers make a hat about his head.
His pulse beat is so slow we think him dead.

He loops in crazy figures half the night
Among the trees that face the corner light.

But when he brushes up against a screen,
We are afraid of what our eyes have seen;

For something is amiss or out of place
When mice with wings can wear a human face.

Theodore Roethke

The tickle rhyme

'Who's that tickling my back?' said the wall.
'Me,' said a small
caterpillar. 'I'm learning
to crawl.'

Ian Serraillier

Rabbits

Rabbits have fur
And also more rabbits
And it is a habit.

A habit is something you are doing
Over and over again
Because you are liking it
When you have it.

A habit of rabbits is having more.
First there is a rabbit with fur
and you have it.
But soon there are more.

Soon they are having more rabbits
Over and over again and liking to do it
And then it is a habit
And rabbits really have it.

Ray Fabrizio

Old Shellover

'Come!' said Old Shellover.
'What?' says Creep.
'The horny old Gardener's fast asleep;
The fat cock Thrush
To his nest has gone;
And the dew shines bright
In the rising Moon;
Old Sallie Worm from her hole doth peep:
Come!' said Old Shellover.
'Ay!' said Creep.

Walter de la Mare

The gnats

The gnats are dancing in the sun,
In vibrant needles of light they run
On the air, and hover in noiseless sound,
Ecstasy ballet, round and around,
Soon for human body bound.

The pin-thin slivers, wingy, white,
Whirl in restless, passionate flight—
Zooming atoms circling, twisting,
Darting, jiving,
Target-diving.
In orbit on orbit of dazzle-gold light,
The gnats are limbering up to bite.

Odette Tchernine

The hairy dog

My dog's so furry I've not seen
His face for years and years:
His eyes are buried out of sight,
I only guess his ears.

When people ask me for his breed,
I do not know or care:
He has the beauty of them all
Hidden beneath his hair.

Herbert Asquith

Tortoise

Lumbering carefully over stone and earth,
  Edging, stumbling, groping blindly,
To the favourite place of Michaelmas daisies.
  His food finished, now the tortoise
Feels his way one foot after another,
  Choosing a path among the grass,
Which looks like willows hovering high above his hard shell.
  Afternoon appears, sleep overpowers the beast.
Making heavy footsteps the tortoise finds a sleeping-place,
  One eye closes and the scum of the eyelid passes over both eyes.
The tortoise falls into a shelled sleep.
  Dawn and he trundles off to find food,
He claws his way over the rockery,
  Which appears to him like the Andes,
Passing through glades of raspberries;
  And at last he finds his food,
Lettuce!
  Clumsily he opens his leather-hard jaws,
Draws his fire-red tongue out,
  Then, with a churning of cranking and creaking efforts,
He closes his mouth upon the lettuce;
  Tortoise now returns and digs with great speed
To hide himself from winter.
  The hole dug, he retreats in his creaking wet-covered shell
To sleep.

David Speechly
(written while at school)

28

To an old cat

She owns a corner by the fire,
Where all the day she sleeps,
She lies there to her heart's desire,
But now and then she peeps
To see what's going on.

A crackle from the burning coal
'Is that a mouse,' she thinks,
'Or someone coming,' not a soul,
So rising off she slinks
To see what she can find.

She finds the pup, he wants to play,
In scorn, puss arches high,
She keeps his frisky paws at bay,
—Although, she wonders why
He does not go away!

Then settling by the fire again,
She yawns, and blinks and stares,
For neither puppy dogs, nor men,
Nor mice, nor me, she cares—
Only to sleep and dream.

Jillian D. Perry, aged 8

The caterpillar

Brown and furry
Caterpillar in a hurry,
Take your walk
To the shady leaf or stalk.

May no toad spy on you,
May the little birds pass by you.
Spin and die,
To live again a butterfly.

Christina Rossetti

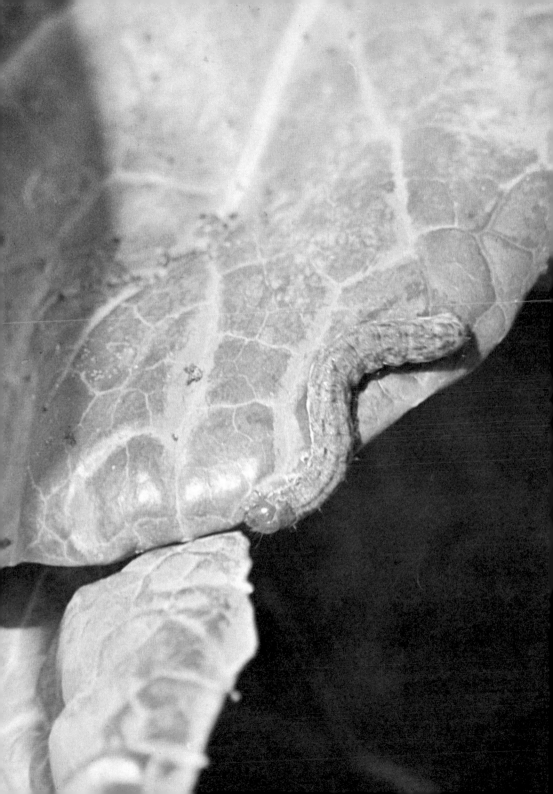

To a squirrel at Kyle-na-no

Come play with me;
Why should you run
Through the shaking tree
As though I'd a gun
To strike you dead?
When all I would do
Is to scratch your head
And let you go.

W. B. Yeats

The snail

At sunset, when the night-dews fall,
Out of the ivy on the wall
With horns outstretched and pointed tail
Comes the grey and noiseless snail.
On ivy stems she clambers down,
Carrying her house of brown.
Safe in the dark, no greedy eye
Can her tender body spy,
While she herself, a hungry thief,
Searches out the freshest leaf.
She travels on as best she can
Like a toppling caravan.

James Reeves

Who's in?

'The door is shut fast
And everyone's out:'
But people don't know
What they're talking about!
Say the fly on the wall,
And the flame on the coals,
And the dog on his rug,
And the mice in their holes,
And the kitten curled up,
And the spiders that spin—
'What, everyone's out?
Why, everyone's in!'

Elizabeth Fleming

Acknowledgements

For permission to reproduce copyright material the Editor and Publishers are indebted to the authors and the following:

William Heinemann Ltd. for 'The hairy dog' by Herbert Asquith and for 'The snail' from *The Wandering Moon* by James Reeves; Blackie and Son Ltd. for 'Who's in?' by Elizabeth Fleming; Mrs. H. M. Davies and Jonathan Cape Ltd. for 'The cat' from *The Complete Poems of W. H. Davies*; Faber & Faber Ltd. and Doubleday & Company Inc. for 'The bat' from *The Collected Poems* by Theodore Roethke; The Macmillan Company for 'The prayer of the mouse' from *Prayers from the Ark* by Carmen Bernos de Gasztold; The Literary Trustees of Walter de la Mare and The Society of Authors for 'Old Shellover' from *The Complete Poems of Walter de la Mare*; The North West Arts Association for 'To an old cat' by Jillian D. Perry from *Young People's Poetry 1970*; Oxford University Press for 'The tickle rhyme' from *The Tale of the Monster Horse* by Ian Serraillier; Odette Tchernine for her poem 'The gnats'; Mr. M. B. Yeats, The Macmillan Company and The Macmillan Company of Canada for 'To a squirrel at Kyle-Na-No' from *The Collected Poems of W. B. Yeats*.

Every effort has been made to trace the owners of copyrights, but we take this opportunity of tendering apologies to any owners whose rights may have been unwittingly infringed.

Weathers and Seasons

Rain

Beautiful rain
Falling so softly
Such a delicate thing

The harvests need you
And some of the flowers
But we too

Because you remind
Of coolness of quiet
Of tenderest words

Come down rain, fall
Not too harshly but give
Your strange sense of peace to us.

Elizabeth Jennings

Spring song

Spring is coming, spring is coming,
   Birdies, build your nest;
Weave together straw and feather,
   Doing each your best.

Spring is coming, spring is coming,
   Flowers are coming too;
Pansies, lilies, daffodillies
   Now are coming through.

Spring is coming, spring is coming,
   All around is fair;
Shimmer and quiver on the river,
   Joy is everywhere.

William Blake

After the storm (an extract)

There was a roaring in the wind all night;
The rain came heavily and fell in floods;
But now the sun is rising calm and bright;
The birds are singing in the distant woods;
Over his own sweet voice the Stock-dove broods;
The Jay makes answer as the Magpie chatters;
And all the air is filled with pleasant noise of waters.

All things that love the sun are out of doors;
The sky rejoices in the morning's birth;
The grass is bright with rain drops; on the moors
The hare is running races in her mirth;
And with her feet she from the plashy earth
Raises a mist; that, glittering in the sun,
Runs with her all the way, wherever she doth run.

William Wordsworth

The wind

Blow, wind, blow today!
Swing the weather-cock round,
Hurry the clouds in the sky away,
And bend the grass to the ground!
Hurry and scurry and puff and blow,
Making the tall trees sway,
I'd like to be with you wherever you go,
Blow, wind, today!

Sherry Ward
(written while at school)

A hot day

Cottonwool clouds loiter.
A lawnmower, very far,
Birrs. Then a bee comes
To a crimson rose and softly,
Deftly and fatly crams
A velvet body in.
A tree, June-lazy, makes
A tent of dim green light.
Sunlight weaves in the leaves,
Honey-light laced with leaf-light,
Green interleaved with gold.
Sunlight gathers its rays
In sheaves, which the wind unweaves
And then reweaves—the wind
That puffs a smell of grass
Through the heat-heavy, trembling
Summer pool of air.

A. S. J. Tessimond

Rainy nights

I like the town on rainy nights
   When everything is wet—
When all the town has magic lights
   And streets of shining jet!

When all the rain about the town
   Is like a looking-glass,
And all the lights are upside-down
   Below me as I pass.

In all the pools are velvet skies,
   And down the dazzling street
A fairy city gleams and lies
   In beauty at my feet.

Irene Thompson

August weather

Dead heat and windless air,
   And silence over all;
Never a leaf astir,
   But the ripe apples fall;
Plums are purple-red,
   Pears amber and brown;
Thud! in the garden-bed!
   Ripe apples fall down.

Air like a cider-press
   With the bruised apples' scent;
Low whistles express
   Some sleepy bird's content;
Still world and windless sky,
   A mist of heat o'er all;
Peace like a lullaby,
   And the ripe apples fall.

Katharine Tynan

The fog

Slowly, the fog,
Hunch-shouldered with a grey face,
Arms wide, advances,
Finger-tips touching the way
Past the dark houses
And dark gardens of roses.
Up the short street from the harbour,
Slowly the fog,
Seeking, seeking;
Arms wide, shoulders hunched,
Searching, searching.
Out through the streets to the fields,
Slowly, the fog—
A blind man hunting the moon.

F. R. McCreary

Autumn for me is

an indescribable earthy smell,
skies palest blue to crimson hue,
mists unravelled by the sun,
spiders' webs sparkling with dew,
a lonely owl hooting in the night,
smoke from bonfires heavenward trailing,
birds' nests looking frayed . . . forgotten,
rose-red apples, ripe and sweet,
wind-whirling, swirling, twirling leaves
bracken-brown undergrowth, heather-covered hills
last petals falling to the ground
last seeds floating—whither bound?
a mellow season
        in between
a golden gleam
        —that's autumn.

Helen Mackay, aged 9

The wind

The wind,
It is a ghostly hand
Pushing to and fro
The leaves and stray paper
That lie scattered in his path.

The trees
Bow down to the strength
Of the whistling wind,
As though paying homage
To some unknown king.

N. Carey, aged 11

A windy day

This wind brings all dead things to life,
Branches that lash the air like whips
And dead leaves rolling in a hurry
Or peering in a rabbit's bury
Or trying to push down a tree;
Gates that fly open to the wind
And close again behind,
And fields that are a flowing sea
And make the cattle look like ships;
Straws glistening and stiff
Lying on air as on a shelf
And pond that leaps to leave itself;
And feathers too that rise and float,
Each feather changed into a bird,
And line-hung sheets that crack and strain;
Even the sun-greened coat,
That through so many winds has served,
The scarecrow struggles to put on again.

Andrew Young

Go out

Go out
When the wind's about;
Let him buffet you
Inside out.

Go out
In a rainy drizzle;
Never sit by the fire
To sizzle.

Go out
When the snowflakes play;
Toss them about
On the white highway.

Go out
And stay till night;
When the sun is shedding
Its golden light.

Eileen Mathias

Snow landscape

Over on the blanketed hill the snow is lighted
   by a dull pink glow, making it look like pink candy floss.
The unfriendly looking trees look stern and
   uninviting against the pink blanket of snow,
   and wear garments of moss.
The long grey limestone wall has fingers of
   splashed slush, stretching over the wall.
It wears a scarf of snow.
Our breath comes in regular foggy clouds and
   dissolves into the thin cold air.
The frosty atmosphere makes our fingers glow.
The castle stands gaunt and desolate and snow
   fringed on the murky freckled hillside.
The trees below it are fringed in a black doyley;
   their branches lace together at the tips.
The roads and the pavement are wet and slushy
   like slimy black snakes.
The snow-capped rooftops make a pattern of white
   squares against the grey shabby houses.
The sky stands vast, like a settling pale blue
   blanket patched with smoky thread.
All around the frosted hills group,
   snow-covered, pink, purple, brown, and white with snow.

Sarah Hollands, aged 10

The eye marvels at the beauty of its whiteness,
   and the mind is amazed at its falling.
He pours the hoarfrost upon the earth like salt,
   and when it freezes, it becomes pointed thorns.
The cold north wind blows,
   and ice freezes over the water;
it rests upon every pool of water,
   and the water puts it on like a breastplate.

Ecclesiasticus xliii, 18–20

Last snow

Although the snow still lingers
Heaped on the ivy's blunt webbed fingers
And painting tree-trunks on one side,
Here in this sunlit ride
The fresh unchristened things appear,
Leaf, spathe and stem,
With crumbs of earth clinging to them
To show the way they came
But no flower yet to tell their name,
And one green spear
Stabbing a dead leaf from below
Kills winter at a blow.

Andrew Young

Acknowledgements

For permission to reproduce copyright material the Editor and Publishers are indebted to the authors and the following:

Leonard Clark for 'Autumn for me is' by Helen Mackay from *Poems by Children*; The Macmillan Company and The Macmillan Company of Canada for 'Rain' from *Lucidities* by Elizabeth Jennings; The North West Arts Association for 'Snow landscape' by Sarah Hollands from *Young People's Poetry 1970*; Routledge & Kegan Paul Ltd. for 'The wind' by N. Carey from *Poems by Children 1950–1961*; The Society of Authors and Miss Pamela Hinkson for 'August weather' by Katharine Tynan; The Andrew Young Estate and Leonard Clark for 'A windy day' and 'Last snow' from *Collected Poems of Andrew Young*.

Every effort has been made to trace the owners of copyrights, but we take this opportunity of tendering apologies to any owners whose rights may have been unwittingly infringed.

Colours

Colours

What is pink? A rose is pink
By the fountain's brink.
What is red? A poppy's red
In its barley bed.
What is blue? The sky is blue
Where the clouds float thro'.
What is white? A swan is white,
Sailing in the light.
What is yellow? Pears are yellow,
Rich and ripe and mellow.
What is green? The grass is green,
With small flowers between.
What is violet? Clouds are violet
In the summer twilight.
What is orange? Why, an orange—
Just an orange!

Christina Rossetti

Counting-out rhyme

Silver bark of beech, and sallow
Bark of yellow birch and yellow
   Twig of willow.

Stripe of green in moosewood maple,
Colour seen in leaf of apple,
   Bark of popple.

Wood of popple pale as moonbeam,
Wood of oak for yoke and barn-beam,
   Wood of hornbeam.

Silver bark of beech, and hollow
Stem of elder, tall and yellow
   Twig of willow.

Edna St. Vincent Millay

The balloons (an extract)

Against these turbid turquoise skies
  The light and luminous balloons
  Dip and drift like satin moons,
Drift like silken butterflies;

Reel with every windy gust,
  Rise and reel like dancing girls,
  Float like strange transparent pearls,
Fall and float like silver dust.

Oscar Wilde

The reaper

Under the dying sun
And the moon's frail shell,
The fields are clear as glass:
I love them well.

A horse's amber flanks
Shine in the grain.
The wheel of the reaper cleaves
A yellow lane.

The reaper is ruddy gold,
Unearthly bright,
Driving an amber cloud,
Touched with its light.

They say the earth's a stone
Wrinkled and old,
Yet she has steeds of fire
And men of gold!

L. H. Allen

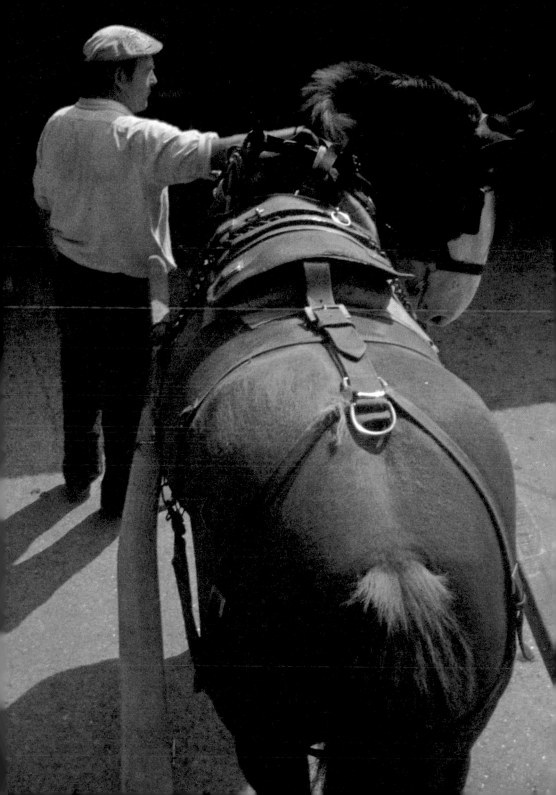

The Rainbow

I saw the lovely arch
Of Rainbow span the sky,
The gold sun burning
As the rain swept by.

In bright-ringed solitude
The showery foliage shone
One lovely moment,
And the Bow was gone.

Walter de la Mare

Shiny

Shiny are the chestnut leaves
Before they unfold.
The inside of a buttercup
Is like polished gold.
A pool in the sunshine
Is bright too,
A silver shilling
When it is new.
But the round full moon,
So clear and white
How brightly she shines
On a winter night!
Slowly she rises,
Higher and higher,
With a cold clear light,
Like ice on fire.

James Reeves

Black

Black the angry colour,
The thunder colour,
The mourning colour,
The black dark underworld.
The creepy frightening colour,
Bare, black trees
Silhouetted against the sky.
The silent night robber
Creeping, creeping,
In the silent black night,
Doing his black deeds.
A fine black stallion
Streaking past.
The black, black darkness.
The raven-black hair,
The raven-black dress.

Black anger of the war,
The cold black damp caves
And the underground caverns.
The angry black cold sea
Reaching,
With its black fingers,
Throwing the forlorn ships
To their black end
On the black rocks
In the black depths of the sea.
Black,
Black, the perilous colour
And black the serious colour.
Black,
The colour of the dead.

Jane Chester aged 11

Red sky at night

Red sky at night,
Shepherd's delight;
Red sky in the morning,
Shepherd's warning.

Traditional

The green spring

When spring comes
I see the woods turning green,
The water in the river turning green,
The hills turning green,
The fields turning green,
The little beetles turning green,
And even the white-bearded old man turning green.
The green blood
Nurtures the fatigued earth,
And from the earth bursts forth
A green hope.

Shan Mei

Spring goeth all in white

Spring goeth all in white,
Crowned with milk-white may:
In fleecy flocks of light
O'er heaven the white clouds stray:

White butterflies in the air;
White daisies prank the ground:
The cherry and hoary pear
Scatter their snow around.

Robert Bridges

What is grey?

Grey is the colour of an elephant
And a mouse
And a tumbledown house.
It's fog and smog,
And very fine print,
It's a hush and
The wetness of melting slush.
Tiredness and oysters
Both are grey,
Smoke swirls
And grandmother's curls.
So are some spring coats
And nanny-goats.
Pigeons are grey
And a rainy day
The sad look of a slum
And chewing gum.
Pussy willows are grey
In a velvety way.
Suits, shoes
And bad news,
Beggars' hats
And alley cats
Skin of a mole
And a worn slipper sole.
Content is grey
And sleepiness, too.
They wear grey suede gloves
When they're touching you . . . . .

Mary O'Neill

Symphony in yellow

An omnibus across the bridge
   Crawls like a yellow butterfly,
   And, here and there, a passer-by
Shows like a little restless midge.

Big barges full of yellow hay
   Are moored against the shadowy wharf,
   And, like a yellow silken scarf,
The thick fog hangs along the quay.

The yellow leaves begin to fade
   And flutter from the Temple elms,
   And at my feet the pale green Thames
Lies like a rod of rippled jade.

Oscar Wilde

No jewel

No jewel from the rock
Is lovely as the dew;
Flashing with flamelike red
With sea-like blue.

No web the merchant weaves
Can rival hers—
The silk the spider spins
Across the furze.

Walter de la Mare

Colours

Red is death, for people who are dying,
Silver is tears, for people who are crying,
Blue is a pool, cool and still,
Green is a beautiful grassy hill.

Grey is for people in the early evening,
Black is a dress for people grieving,
Brown is for an old queen's gown,
Gold for a princess's crown.

Frances Evans

Chameleon

I can think sharply
and I can change:
my colours cover a considerable range.

I can be some mud by
an estuary,
I can be a patch on the bark of a tree.

I can be green grass
or a little thin stone
—or if I really want to be left alone,

I can be a shadow . . .
What I am on your
multi-coloured bedspread, I am not quite sure.

Alan Brownjohn

Acknowledgements

For permission to reproduce copyright material the Editor and Publishers are indebted to the authors and the following:

The Clarendon Press for 'Spring goeth all in white' from *The Shorter Poems of Robert Bridges*; Doubleday & Company, Inc. for 'The green spring' from *Shepherding Winds* by Shan Mei; The Hamlyn Publishing Group Ltd. for 'Black' by Jane Chester from *Following the Sun*; The Literary Trustees of Walter de la Mare and the Society of Authors for 'No jewel' and 'The Rainbow' from *The Complete Poems of Walter de la Mare 1969*; The Macmillan Company for 'Chameleon' from *Brownjohn's Beasts* by Alan Brownjohn; Norma Millay Ellis and Harper & Row for 'Counting-out rhyme' from *Collected Poems by Edna St. Vincent Millay*; William Heinemann Ltd. for 'Shiny' from *The Wandering Moon* by James Reeves; Frederick Warne & Co. for 'Colours' from *Round About Eight* by Frances Evans; World's Work Ltd. and Doubleday & Company Inc. for 'What is grey?' from *Hailstones and Halibut Bones* by Mary O'Neill.

Every effort has been made to trace the owners of copyrights, but we take this opportunity of tendering apologies to any owners whose rights may have been unwittingly infringed.

Sea and Shore

Grim and gloomy

Oh, grim and gloomy,
So grim and gloomy
Are the caves beneath the sea.
Oh, rare but roomy
And bare and boomy,
Those salt sea caverns be.

Oh, slim and slimy
Or grey and grimy
Are the animals of the sea.
Salt and oozy
And safe and snoozy
The caves where those animals be.

Hark to the shuffling,
Huge and snuffling,
Ravenous, cavernous,
great sea-beasts!
But fair and fabulous,
Tintinnabulous,
Gay and fabulous are their feasts.

Ah, but the queen of the sea,
The querulous, perilous sea!
How the curls of her tresses
The pearls on her dresses,
Sway and swirl in the waves,
How cosy and dozy,
How sweet ring-a-rosy
Her bower in the deep-sea caves!

Oh, rare but roomy
And bare and boomy
Those caverns under the sea,
And grave and grandiose,
Safe and sandiose
The dens of her denizens be.

James Reeves

The waves of the sea

Don't you go too near the sea,
  The sea is sure to wet you.
Harmless though she seems to be
  The sea's ninth wave will get you!
But I can see the small white waves
  That want to play with me—
They won't do more than wet my feet
  When I go near the sea.

Don't you go too near the sea,
  She does not love a stranger.
Eight untroubled waves has she,
  The ninth is full of danger!
But I can see the smooth blue waves
  That want to play with me—
They won't do more than wet my knees
  When I go near the sea.

Don't you go too near the sea,
  She'll set her waves upon you.
Eight will treat you playfully,
  Until the ninth has won you.
But I can see the big green waves
  That want to play with me—
They won't do more than wet my waist
  When I go near the sea.

Don't you go too near the sea,
  Her ways are full of wonder.
Her first eight waves will leave you free,
  Her ninth will take you under!
But I can see the great grey waves
  That want to play with me—
They won't do more than wet my neck
  When I go near the sea.

Don't you go too near the sea—
  O Child, you set me quaking!
Eight have passed you silently,
  And now the ninth is breaking!
I see a wave as high as a wall
  That wants to play with me—
O Mother, O Mother, it's taken me all,
  For I went too near the sea!

Eleanor Farjeon

The pool in the rock

In this water, clear as air,
Lurks a lobster in its lair.
Rock-bound weed sways out and in,
Coral-red, and bottle-green.
Wondrous pale anemones
Stir like flowers in a breeze:
Fluted scallop, whelk in shell,
And the prowling mackerel.
Winged with snow the sea-mews ride
The brine-keen wind; and far and wide
Sounds on the hollow thunder of the tide.

Walter de la Mare

Sea shell

Sea Shell, Sea Shell,
Sing me a song, O Please!
A song of ships, and sailor men,
And parrots, and tropical trees,

Of islands lost in the Spanish Main
Which no man ever may find again,
Of fishes and corals under the waves,
And sea horses stabled in great green caves.

Sea Shell, Sea Shell,
Song of the things you know so well.

Amy Lowell

Seaside

Barefoot on the hard wet sand
Run and run,
The world is just awake, stretching
In the sun.
As far as we can see, the beach lies
New and clean
Shining with stones and shells, jewels
For a Queen.

Look, a starfish rocking gently
In a pool.
Catch it—put it back again
Safe and cool.
Play until the tide comes up
Foaming white
To wash the sand smooth again
In the night.

Jennifer Andrews

A flock of little boats

A flock of little boats
Tethered to the shore
Drifts in still water . . .
Prows dip, nibbling.

Samuel Menashe

My seashell

My pretty little seashell—
I keep it safe and dry.
Yet once down at the seashore,
In water it used to lie.

My Grandad
From the Black Sea
Has brought it to me;
And if you listen closely,
You'll hear in it the sea.

You'll hear in it the breakers,
The hissing of the foam,
And you will think the Black Sea
Has come into your home.

Agnia Barto
Translated by M. Morton

The diver

I would like to dive
Down
Into this still pool
Where the rocks at the bottom are safely deep,

Into the green
Of the water seen from within,
A strange light
Streaming past my eyes—

Things hostile,
You cannot stay here, they seem to say;
The rocks, slime-covered, the undulating
Fronds of weeds—

And drift slowly
Among the cooler zones;
Then, upward turning,
Break from the green glimmer

Into the light,
White and ordinary, of day,
And the mild air,
With the breeze and the comfortable shore.

W. W. E. Ross

The sea

The sea is a hungry dog,
Giant and grey.
He rolls on the beach all day.
With his clashing teeth and shaggy jaws
Hour upon hour he gnaws
The rumbling, tumbling stones,
And 'Bones, bones, bones, bones!'
The giant sea-dog moans,
Licking his greasy paws.

And when the night wind roars
And the moon rocks in the stormy cloud,
He bounds to his feet and snuffs and sniffs,
Shaking his wet sides over the cliffs,
And howls and hollows long and loud.

But on quiet days in May or June,
When even the grasses on the dune
Play no more their reedy tune,
With his head between his paws
He lies on the sandy shores,
So quiet, so quiet, he scarcely snores.

James Reeves

Coral grove (an extract)

Deep in the wave is a coral grove,
Where the purple mullet and gold-fish rove;
Where a sea flower spreads its leaves of blue
That never are wet with falling dew,
But in bright and changeful beauty shine
Far down in the green and glassy brine.
The floor is of sand, like the mountain drift,
And the pearl-shells spangle the flinty snow;
From coral rocks the sea plants lift
Their boughs, where the tides and billows flow;
The water is calm and still below,
For the winds and waves are absent there,
And the sands are bright as the stars that glow.

James Gates Percival

The tide rises, the tide falls

The tide rises, the tide falls,
The twilight darkens, the curlew calls;
Along the sea-sands damp and brown
The traveller hastens toward the town,
   And the tide rises, the tide falls.

Darkness settles on roofs and walls,
But the sea, the sea in the darkness calls;
The little waves, with their soft, white hands,
Efface the footprints in the sands,
   And the tide rises, the tide falls.

The morning breaks; the steeds in their stalls
Stamp and neigh, as the hostler calls;
The day returns, but nevermore
Returns the traveller to the shore,
   And the tide rises, the tide falls.

Henry Wadsworth Longfellow

Under the sea

Watch!
What is it you see?

The crimson tentacles of a Squid;
Beyond them the misty darkness of the deep.
Misty, misty, the darkness of the deep,
And blue like dark blue ink.

Did you hear?
What did you hear?

The deep gurgle of dislodging coral;
Beyond it the eternal silence of the deep.
Silent, silent, the eternal silence of the deep,
And blue like dark blue ink.

Oh, search!
What is it you see?

Young golden little lobsters,
Scavenging, developing enormous claws.
Free, free in the vastness of the deep,
Like the deepest blue ink.

Dive deeper! dive deeper!

Alan Butterfield, aged 12

128

The main-deep

The long-rólling,
Steady-póuring,
Deep-trenchéd
Green billów:

The wide-topped,
Unbróken,
Green-glacid,
Slow-sliding,

Cold-flushing,
—On—on—on—
Chill-rushing,
Hush-hushing,

. . . . . Hush-hushing . . . . .

James Stephens

A deserted beach

Silently the little Crab crawled along the beach,
　　The wind howls,
　　The Crab rolls over,
　　He hits a rock,
　　The Crab lies still,
　　There is no movement . . .
　　He is dead.
　　The beach is deserted, empty.

Where are the Sea-gulls and Oysters?
Where are the Cockles and Mussels?
Where are the Sandcastles?

They have been there,
But now . . . they have gone,
Where have they gone?
Nobody knows . . .
Except the greedy sea.

Robin Smallman
(Written while at school)

All day I hear the noise of waters

All day I hear the noise of waters
   Making moan,
Sad as the sea-bird is, when going
   Forth alone,
He hears the winds cry to the waters'
   Monotone.
The grey winds, the cold winds are blowing
   Where I go.
I hear the noise of many waters
   Far below.
All day, all night, I hear them flowing
   To and fro.

James Joyce

Acknowledgements

For permission to reproduce copyright material the Editor and Publishers are indebted to the authors and the following:

The Executors of the James Joyce Estate and Jonathan Cape Ltd. for 'All day I hear the noise of waters' from *Chamber Music* by James Joyce; William Heinemann Ltd. for 'Grim and gloomy' and 'The sea' from *The Wandering Moon* by James Reeves; Houghton Mifflin Company for 'Sea Shell' from *The Complete Poetical Works of Amy Lowell*; The Literary Trustees of Walter de la Mare and The Society of Authors for 'The pool in the rock' from *The Complete Poems of Walter de la Mare 1969*; Longman Canada Ltd. for 'The diver' from *Shapes & Sounds* by W. W. E. Ross; Samuel Menashe for his poem 'A flock of little boats' from *The Many Named Beloved*; The North West Arts Association for 'Under the sea' by Alan Butterfield from *Young People's Poetry 1970*; Oxford University Press for 'The waves of the sea' from *The Children's Bells* by Eleanor Farjeon; Robin Smallman for his poem 'A deserted beach' from *As Large as Alone*; Mrs Iris Wise, The Macmillan Company and The Macmillan Company of Canada for 'The main-deep' from *Collected Poems* by James Stephens; Jennifer Andrews for her poem 'Seaside'.

Every effort has been made to trace the owners of copyrights, but we take this opportunity of tendering apologies to any owners whose rights may have been unwittingly infringed.